The Executive Guide to Impl
Accounting Software

The Executive Guide to Implementing Accounting Software

Over 100 Ways to Ensure the Success of Your Project

Ken E. Sebahar

2007

Introduction

In my many years implementing enterprise resource planning (ERP) and accounting software packages at well over one hundred small and mid-sized organizations, I have found one common denominator that defines organizations that successfully implement these packages—they take ownership of the new software. Many elements constitute taking ownership of software, and I present them here as simple and concise recommendations that you can follow as you navigate through your own implementation project. Overall, "taking ownership" means realizing that your organization is responsible for managing the implementation project and ensuring that the software will meet the current and future requirements of the organization.

This guide is for anyone who is currently in the midst of an ERP or accounting software implementation or who is considering purchasing such a package. Executives, consultants, accountants, and others will benefit from this guide by applying the best practices and recommendations presented to their existing projects and implementations.

You can find many reference books on the market today that may be helpful in managing an accounting software implementation; however, these books typically fall into one of two categories—general project management references or vendor-specific user references. The general project management references do a thorough job of explaining the general concepts and techniques used in managing a large project, but they fall short in covering the specific elements that make an accounting software implementation unique. The vendor-specific references explain how a specific vendor's software functions, but these references are typically very complex and do not provide executive guidance on how to manage the *implementation* of the software from an organizational perspective.

This guide provides executive-level guidance throughout all phases of the implementation project. It will help ensure the success of any accounting software implementation by providing specific practical steps that you can take as you progress through the project.

For years, many types of organizations have applied the concepts in this guide to successfully implement new ERP and accounting software packages. Until now, however, no one has consolidated and packaged these concepts for quick reference by the business executive. I have tried to keep this guide general in nature so that organizations can apply the concepts to the implementation of any ERP or accounting software package. While these concepts relate to many types of business system implementations (including full ERP implementations, financial accounting implementations, job-costing system implementations, manufacturing system implementations, or other types of business management systems), for the purposes of this guide, the general term "software" will be used where applicable as each of the concepts is presented.

The layout of this guide specifically addresses the busy nature of a typical executive or project manager. Accordingly, you will find a chapter for each major phase of an accounting software implementation, allowing for quick reference based on the current stage of the project. I present several concepts in each chapter as directly and concisely as possible. Each of the concepts includes two parts: 1) a quick-reference title/summary followed by, 2) a more detailed explanation of the concept. These are the concepts that allow you to take ownership of your implementation project. Once your organization feels a true sense of ownership and responsibility, you are well on your way to a successful implementation of your new software.

Chapter 1

Software Evaluation

The evaluation phase of a software implementation begins with a determination that the organization may require new software and usually ends with the purchase of the new software. Regardless of how long this process takes, the organization must complete several key process-related tasks to ensure successful implementation of the software.

Software Evaluation

Defining the Project Vision

Create and share your vision.

Create a vision of how the new software will impact the organization. Then, share this vision with all project team members. This vision should include the ways in which the new software will improve efficiencies, provide for better communication with other users, vendors, and customers, or provide for better reporting and analysis of financial data. The implementation of new software should also be viewed as an opportunity to change the current processes in order to improve efficiencies and user satisfaction.

Software Evaluation

Defining the Project Vision

Create a "must have" features list.

Define the core requirements of the new software by listing no more than ten essential "must have" features. These "must have" features should be mandatory requirements for any new software you are considering. To avoid confusion with features that are not mandatory, make a second "wish list" of features. These "wish list" features are those things that would be nice to have, but are not deal-breakers if *not* available with one of the software packages you are evaluating. You can expect that many of the software packages under consideration will have all of the basic features you require, so focus on the things that are specific to your business and make sure these are on the list.

Software Evaluation

Defining the Project Vision

Be open to new ways to accomplish the same goal.

If your plan is to replace your current software with new software that *mirrors what you have now*, then be prepared to invest substantially in having to program customizations to the new software prior to deploying it within your organization. A much more reasonable plan is to accept that the new software will most likely function differently than the existing software. The focus during the evaluation phase should be to ensure that the end result is what you need despite the differences in how it may handle specific processes. Users are very dynamic, and despite the initial frustrations of learning a new process, they will quickly learn the new procedure and will appreciate the ways in which the new software improves their daily activities.

Software Evaluation

Setting the Project Budget

Accept the 1:1 ratio.

A widely held rule of thumb is that for each dollar spent on software licensing and maintenance over the first three years of software use, you will spend one additional dollar in consulting services to implement the new software. Despite significant improvements made by software vendors in the tools used to implement new software, any consulting services proposal provided by a vendor that is signficantly less than that 1:1 ratio may be overly optimistic. If the proposed ratio of services to software is not 1:1, ask specifically what measures the software vendor has taken to reduce the "industry standard" requirements for implementation services. In a fully integrated manufacturing or job-costing environment, a minimum 2:1 services-to-software ratio should be planned if the typical functions are to be implemented. While these ratios are a good starting point for estimating a project budget, the project requirements discovered during the software evaluation phase may result in a ratio that is very different from the initial estimate. Do not be surprised if the proposed ratio is higher than 1:1, as many software packages contain advanced features requiring significant professional assistance to configure and implement. Additional aspects of an implementation project that may drastically skew this ratio include complex data conversion requirements, a high level of customization to the software, and any processes within your organization where the new software will be used to replace manual procedures. Finally, a high ratio may be the result of discounts being applied to the purchase price of the software licenses.

Software Evaluation

Setting the Project Budget

Financing is a great way to get the new software up and running right now.

A typical scenario is that an organization makes a determination that new software is required as soon as possible due to expansion of the business or the instability of the existing software. However, this significant expenditure may not have been in the budget, and there may be no cash flow to support such a project. Instead of putting the overdue project on hold until next year or beyond, consider financing the entire software implementation. Most financial institutions and lenders will allow you to finance the hardware, software, and even services, although typically the services require a higher interest rate. Selecting a three-year financing term will allow the investment to be repaid over three years, easing or even eliminating the burden of the project from a cash-flow perspective and allowing the organization to focus on what is most important—completing the project.

Software Evaluation

Setting the Project Budget

Compare apples to apples.

Often it is difficult to compare the total costs of each software package being evaluated because of the varying ways software vendors price their products. For example, some software vendors will provide a price per concurrent user (number of users logged onto the software at the same time), others price per module, while still others price per month or per year. Regardless of the pricing structure utilized, for a true comparison of total software costs, prepare and review a three-year investment summary for each software package being evaluated. This will provide a more accurate method for comparing the total investment required for all software packages being evaluated.

Software Evaluation

Setting the Project Budget

Don't stretch your budget before the project even starts.

During the software evaluation period, many users fall in love with the "bells and whistles" vendors typically demonstrate. However, often these bells and whistles are not even included within your original core requirements "must have" list or even your "wish list." Usually it is the higher-end software that offers these tantalizing flashy features. When possible, avoid purchasing software if the initial license price is at the high end of your budget range. If you do decide to purchase the high-end software, be sure you can list the legitimate business reasons why only this software will benefit your organization. Besides the additional up-front investment in software licensing, it is likely that the initial implementation costs as well as the ongoing maintenance and support costs will be higher than originally anticipated.

Software Evaluation

Setting the Project Budget

It is better to invest more on software that you are confident you can successfully implement than to invest less in software in which you have less confidence.

While it is important to make sure that the software selected fits into your short- and long-range budgeting, a common mistake is purchasing software with a lower price tag even though you have more doubts about successfully implementing it at your organization. The investment in terms of time and money is too great to risk being unable to successfully deploy the software. Thus, if you find software that makes you both comfortable with its features and confident you will achieve on-time, on-budget implementation, it is definitely worth any additional investment (within reason, of course). One or two years after the implementation project has been completed successfully, it will be of little consequence that the software required a slightly higher investment than others you considered during the evaluation phase.

Software Evaluation

Setting the Project Budget

Purchase only the software licenses that you need today.

If the software you want allows purchasing by module or by user, purchase only those modules or those user licenses that you are confident will be implemented immediately. Your intentions of implementing additional modules or users in the future may change after the initial deployment of the software. Common causes of altered plans include: the difficulty of implementing the software; changes to the business requirements; advancement of newer technologies as the project progresses; or management changes regarding the future direction of the company in terms of business policies or use of technology. It is rare that a software vendor will provide a credit or "return" if the software or user licenses are not deployed, so do not over-purchase prior to implementing the core functionality required by your organization.

Software Evaluation

Planning and Attending Demonstrations

Grade the software vendors' ability to follow an agenda and execute it well.

Prior to attending each software demonstration, provide each vendor with an agenda detailing the specific processes to be reviewed during the demonstration. Rate each vendor's ability to successfully complete each requested transaction as well as the ability to understand your requirements and follow your agenda. In addition to selecting new software, you are also selecting a new business partner who will assist your organization with the implementation and support of your new software. Thus, it is important that this new partner is able to understand your business and apply this knowledge during the demonstration (and eventual implementation) of the software. Very often, the software will provide multiple alternatives to accomplish the same goal, and a competent consulting partner will be able to recommend the best alternative for *your* organization.

Software Evaluation

Planning and Attending Demonstrations

Seeing is believing!

In order to select the correct software for your organization, it is important to understand which processes are key to your business. While evaluating software, ask to see a live demonstration of each of your key business processes from start to finish so that you can see how each process will be accomplished in the new software. This does not mean that you should ask to see a demonstration of every process performed by your users. Instead, focus on the key processes that make your business unique and provide your competitive advantage. For any processes that were *not* specficially addressed during the product demonstration, do not be surprised by how the purchased software completes a specific task, as each software package has its own way of completing common processes. While all software will typically result in the same "bottom line," they will get to this result in their own unique way.

Software Evaluation

Software or Vendor References

Focus your reference checks to maximize their value.

Prior to purchasing the new software, ask the vendor to provide at least three references — and then check them. The goal of contacting the references is to ensure that the team implementing your new software has successfully done so at other organizations. Therefore, ask for references from the last three customers whose software was implemented by the team that will be implementing your new software. Asking for the last three is important because it will assist in eliminating references running old versions of the software. This method may also eliminate references implemented by consultants who are no longer employed by the vendor. If adequate telephone calls are made to the provided references, a visit to the reference's place of business should not be required. Site visits typically do not provide the expected value and can result in an uncomfortable environment as your team intrudes on another business that in turn receives little or no benefit from allowing visitors to tour their facility.

Software Evaluation

Software or Vendor References

Ask the references where the software or implementation process did not meet their expectations.

When contacting software vendor references, be sure to ask not only how their organizations perceived the implementation, but also what elements of the implementation process could have been better. Also, ask how their organization's eventual use of the software differed from their initial expectations at the time of purchase. If you are implementing software that is not widely known or is focused on your specific industry, then reference checks that focus on specific software features are very important to ensure that the software is complete and stable. However, if your organization operates a fairly standard set of transactions and the software being considered is widely used, the reference checks should be less focused on the software and more focused on the vendor's performance during and beyond the implementation.

Software Evaluation

Software or Vendor References

Ask for an "upgrade" reference.

Purchasing new software is a major investment, and it is critical that this investment be utilized for as long a period as possible. Thus, it is important to ensure that the software can be upgraded to the latest release for a reasonable fee. Many software packages allow customization of the software, but these customizations make upgrading to a newer version of the software difficult if not impossible. Ask the software vendor for at least one reference who has recently completed an upgrade to a recent version. This reference will assist in gauging the possibility, difficulty, and cost of upgrading the software to the latest version once you have been up and running on the new software for a period of time.

Software Evaluation

Software or Vendor References

Meet the vendor's project manager before purchasing the software.

Once the software has been selected but prior to purchasing it, request a meeting with your new implementation consultant. You must be comfortable with this individual's personality and knowledge of the software. This individual will have a signficant impact on the success of your project. If you do not feel comfortable with this individual, now is the time to request a different project manager or for some assurances regarding the individual's performance prior to beginning the project. While it may be uncomfortable sharing your concerns with the vendor, it will open a dialogue regarding the individual's experience and knowledge of the software and may alleviate your initial concerns. If doubts still persist, an acceptable plan is to agree with the vendor's management on a formal method for monitoring the progress of the implementation and making adjustments in the future if you need a new consultant.

Chapter 2

Module Selection

One of the complexities of purchasing new software is determining which modules or features are included within each software package. Additionally, while many software packages will contain a wide range of modules, it is important to understand which of these various modules your organization requires.

Module Selection

Implementing Specific Applications

The general ledger account structure will determine your ability to analyze data.

General ledger (G/L): This is the core of any ERP or accounting software package. Most functionality is standard among software packages, but a focal point during the evaluation phase should be the flexibility of the G/L account structure and definition. The G/L account flexibility determines how all sales, purchases, and manufacturing transactions flow to the financial statements, which in turn determines the level of flexibility in analyzing the organization's performance. Financial statements are the tools that provide your organization with the information essential to manage and grow the organization. Thus, it is important to ensure up front that the transactions processed on a daily basis through the software result in complete and detailed financial statements.

Module Selection

Implementing Specific Applications

"Financials" are not all the same.

Payables, receivables, and other standard financial modules: These modules are frequently overlooked during the evaluation phase because a common misconception is that "financials are financials." To a degree this is true, but if you elect not to review the specific functionality of these modules during the demonstration and evaluation phase, do not be surprised if the software processes transactions differently than you anticipated once you are trained on how these modules function. Stay focused on making sure that your required business processes can be completed, and be willing to adapt to how the software completes these common processes.

Module Selection

Implementing Specific Applications

CRM should be integrated with the back-office accounting software "out of the box." If CRM is new to the organization, implement it after the initial deployment of the software.

Customer relationship management (CRM): CRM assists the organization in managing the sales team's activities and in reviewing a customer's history and profile. An integrated CRM module is a great benefit, since one software package can be used to provide organization-wide access to the sales pipeline and customer interaction history. Converting from a manual method of managing customer relationships to CRM software is a major cultural change for any organization. Thus, if your organization is not currently using an integrated CRM solution, deploy this module only after you have completed the initial deployment of the new accounting software.

Module Selection

Implementing Specific Applications

Job costing functionality is critical for those organizations that produce unique products or services. Ensure that you are comfortable with how the profitability is calculated.

Job costing: Job costing consists of tracking all revenue and costs associated with a specific customer sale or job. Typical job costs include labor, materials, freight, service fees, and subcontracting expenses. There are many software packages available that have been designed specifically to handle the special requirements of a job costing organization, and these packages should be considered if job costing is the primary component of the organization. However, if job costing is not a major component of the organization, it may not warrant purchasing software to handle these specific requirements. This is especially so if a general software package can handle the majority of the job costing requirements. If you are doing job costing today, be clear on how the new software calculates job profitability so that you can decide either to adapt your organization's practices to the new software or to modify the new software to accomplish the required results.

Module Selection

Implementing Specific Applications

Save time and money by utilizing the software's standard document formats.

Document formatting: The formatting of printed documents, such as purchase orders and sales invoices, helps communicate your organization's image to your business partners. However, often there is too much focus placed in this area, which negatively impacts the budget and timeline of the implementation project. Plan on using the formats provided by the new software. Utilize what already exists if generally acceptable, and modify the existing documents only to add the required data that is missing from the standard document format. The overall emphasis should be placed on ensuring that the software-generated documents communicate the intended message in a clear and concise manner to your business partners.

Module Selection

Implementing Specific Applications

Document imaging software packages are a great organizational tool if a business case exists.

Document imaging solutions: These software packages are typically independent applications that integrate with ERP or accounting software packages. Although the feature list varies widely between products, their primary function creates the ability to electronically store and re-create images of documents such as signed quotes, purchase orders, delivery tickets, or invoices. These packages can have a significant impact on the overall efficiencies of your organization; however, a specific business purpose must exist to justify the cost of purchasing and implementing this type of package.

Module Selection

Implementing Specific Applications

EDI should be implemented only when mandated by a business partner or in very high volume transaction environments. An EDI administrator will be required.

Electronic data interchange (EDI): Many customers or vendors in high-volume transaction environments will request that you communicate with them electronically in order to transact business more efficiently. EDI allows computers to communicate directly with one another, thus eliminating the need to manually key transactions into your software package. Often, implementing an integrated EDI solution requires a significant up-front investment as well as access to an individual who can administer this electronic communication software. This module should be implemented only if mandated by a key customer or vendor, or when the volume of transactions justifies this improved efficiency.

Module Selection

Implementing Specific Applications

Track fixed assets in the software only if asset tracking is a critical aspect of the organization's business.

Fixed assets: Many small and mid-sized businesses have outside accounting firms track and manage depreciation of their fixed assets. This is the recommended solution when there are a small number of fixed assets or when the accounting staff is not trained in fixed asset management. Purchasing a fixed asset module with your new accounting software will provide a signficant benefit if you purchase and maintain a high number of assets and if the internal accounting staff is trained in proper accounting methods for fixed assets for both corporate and tax purposes. If you infrequently purchase fixed assets, and you require an asset depreciation calculation only at year-end, then implementing a fixed assets module may not provide an acceptable return on investment.

Module Selection

Implementing Specific Applications

Advanced warehouse automation can transform an organization, but it often restricts the flexibility a dynamic organization requires.

Advanced warehouse management: In a high-volume warehouse where each member of the staff is assigned a specific role (i.e., receiving, packing, shipping, or returns), automation of the warehouse via advanced warehouse management software can significantly improve operational efficiencies and radically increase the accuracy of inventory counts and transactions. This is especially true when utilizing radio-frequency or wireless barcoding devices. However, many small to mid-sized organizations simply do not have the organizational structure or discipline required to implement an advanced warehouse management module that allows directed picking, put-away, and warehouse movements by bin. Many times, the primary benefit of instructing the warehouse staff on when and where to move inventory is simply not realized in a small to mid-sized warehouse where the staff already has an intimate understanding of the existing customer and inventory history. A general rule of thumb is that you do not need an automated warehouse system if most of your staff knows where most of the products sit in the warehouse most of the time.

Module Selection

Implementing Specific Applications

In order to recoup the costs of implementing wireless bar-coding, a large transaction volume is required.

Bar-code processing: The addition of bar-coding devices will significantly improve operational efficiencies within the warehouse or shop floor, especially in a serialized-inventory environment. Providing users with the ability to scan a bar code, either in receiving, shipping, or for completing physical inventory counts, will improve accuracy, efficiency, and employee morale. However, wireless hardware, communication tools, and software implementation services require a significant up-front investment to get a wireless environment up and running. If you are a small to medium-sized business, do not attempt to replicate what large organizations like UPS and FedEx are doing with these technologies. UPS and FedEx currently leverage wireless and bar-code technologies very well, but they also invested several million dollars to deploy their current technology architecture, and they spend millions more annually to maintain these software applications. Focus the use of bar coding on the one or two key processes that will provide the highest return on investment. Electing to implement bar-code devices that are wired to the existing workstations in the warehouse will signficantly decrease the hardware investment when compared to radio-frequency or other wireless devices.

Module Selection

Implementing Specific Applications

Integrating your shipping software with the accounting software can provide signficant efficiencies in high-volume shipping environments.

Integrated shipping solution: Integrating your accounting software with a third-party shipping system (such as UPS or FedEx) can result in significantly improved operations and customer service due to the ability to efficiently process and track your customers' packages. Integrating accounting software to a shipping system for the first time typically requires significant time, investment, and testing prior to deployment. In addition, your organization must have an internal staff member who is familiar with the integration for general support and maintenance. Carefully evaluate the number of packages shipped per day (and per carrier) to determine if integration will provide an adequate return on investment. Ascertain how much time is saved per package, and annualize this savings to determine how long it will take to recoup the initial investment.

Module Selection

Implementing Specific Applications

Human resource modules have little integration with other accounting modules, and the sensitive nature of the information must be considered.

Human resources: Generally speaking, having fewer software packages means greater efficiencies and less maintenance time and expense. However, because there is typically no integration with other accounting modules and because of the sensative nature of employee information, human resource information can be left off-line or in a stand-alone software package. You must determine whether it is essential to track employee information within the new accounting software. If you have a current stand-alone human resource software package that performs well and is utilizing current technology, consider continuing the use of this software. After the initial deployment of the accounting software, you can evaluate how the functionality of the new software's human resource module compares to the existing software. At that time, the data can be transitioned to the new software.

Module Selection

Implementing Specific Applications

Under one hundred employees? Outsource payroll. Outsourcing should also be considered if you have over one hundred employees.

Payroll: Payroll outsourcing firms have become quite efficient at processing payroll transactions. This, along with increased competition in the payroll outsourcing industry, has led to an overall decrease in the typical payroll processing fee. All firms with fewer than one hundred employees should outsource payroll processing. This is because the per-employee cost of implementing, maintaining, and running payroll internally (don't forget the cost of your employees' time to manage the payroll process) will almost always be higher than the per-employee cost of outsourcing the payroll service. If you have more than one hundred employees, there is still a good argument to outsource payroll due to the complexities involved in tax and deduction tracking, tax rate maintenance, and year-end tax and compliance reporting.

Module Selection

Implementing Specific Applications

An online storefront? Yes.
An online storefront integrated with your back-office accounting
software? Maybe.

Integrated Web site: An online storefront for your business can be a significant growth opportunity and customer retention tool. For many organizations, an online storefront is essential, but the volume of transactions is not signficant. Real-time integration between your Web site and accounting software is a powerful solution, but you should be sure that a proper budget has been set, including the recurring annual budget for ongoing Web site administration and support. Remember, the image of your organization is defined by what your customer sees on your Web site, not whether or not you have integrated the Web site with your accounting software.

Chapter 3

Working with the Software Vendor

Every single software implementation project is unique.
Although the vendor has successfully implemented the software
many times in the past, no two projects have been the same. Your
organization's implementation project will be successful only if
your project team can communicate effectively with the vendor
and if you are willing to take ownership of the project and the
new software.

Working with the Software Vendor

Managing the Budget

Actively manage the budget.

Your organization is responsible for managing the implementation of the new software, and this includes managing the budget. While the vendor may provide regular budget updates and reports, do not assume that the vendor will proactively ensure that the software is implemented within the estimated budget. In order to ensure that the project costs do not spiral too far upward, review the progress of the implementation against the budget weekly or biweekly to verify that progress made is commesurate with the budget being used. Also, address any budgetary concerns with the software vendor immediately to set the expectation early that managing the budget is important to your organization.

Working with the Software Vendor

Managing the Budget

Make sure you know when the "meter is running."

Software vendors typically bill their services either on an hourly basis (also known as a "time-and-materials basis") or as a fixed-fee basis (all implementation services are provided for one lump sum amount). Understand how your vendor charges for time against the implementation project. The vendor should welcome the opportunity to establish guidelines for how services will be billed to your organization. The vendor may be willing to negotiate alternative arrangements if you have a legitimate reason to deviate from their standard billing policies and procedures.

Working with the Software Vendor

Managing the Budget

Volunteer your services at each opportunity.

Before your software vendor begins any new project task, ask if there are any elements of the task that your project team can complete. This approach will provide your team with a greater sense of project ownership—and will reduce your project budget. Ultimately, this proactive approach also leads to a greater likelihood of project success because your project team has become familiar with the setup and testing of the software throughout the implementation and will be available to assist other users throughout the deployment phase, all making for a smooth transition to the new software.

Working with the Software Vendor

Managing the Budget

Review each service invoice as soon as it is received.

When utilizing a software vendor to assist with the implementation, invoices for installation and training services will most likely arrive early and often as the project gets underway. As soon as each invoice arrives, make sure that every task listed on the invoice has been completed as stated. Do not wait until the project is over budget or behind schedule to review the individual invoices or the total budget. The vendor should provide periodic updates of the budget, but keep in mind that while the vendor wants you to be a happy customer who is willing to serve as a reference once the project is completed, the vendor will inherently welcome any requests your organization submits for additional services above and beyond the original project scope. Thus, it is best to be proactive in managing your implementation project budget. Most software vendors rely on their reputations and will therefore be professional and ethical in every effort. However, this is your accounting software implementation, so you must closely manage the implementation.

Working with the Software Vendor

Managing the Budget

Link each implementation task with a tangible project step.

Each task performed by the software vendor should be accompanied by a clearly distinguishable result or delivered document. This link helps ensure that each step, task, and phase of the project is carried out according to the budget and adds value to the project. While this is also a good practice for managing your project team's progress, it is more important to track results of the software vendor, as the vendor is typically billing for services against your project budget and the cost of each task directly correlates with the overall budget.

Working with the Software Vendor

Proper Communication Techniques

Coordinate all communication with the vendor through one person.

To effectively manage the communication between your organization and the software vendor, assign one individual to be your project manager. This project manager will be responsible for communicating directly with the vendor's project manager. This primary channel for all communication helps to eliminate miscommunication and redundant work by multiple team members. It also provides a structure for communicating issues and concerns between parties.

Working with the Software Vendor

Proper Communication Techniques

Overcommunicate and ask questions often — after all, you don't do this every day.

Overcommunicate and ask the software vendor questions often throughout the implementation project. Without proper communication, assumptions are made and tasks are not completed as expected. Do not be afraid to ask questions and overcommunicate with the software vendor during this project. An organization typically implements new software every five to ten years, so one cannot be expected to be an expert on the process of implementing new software. Lean on the vendor to guide your organization through this project, but also use your knowledge of your organization and project team to define the flow of the project.

Working with the Software Vendor

Proper Communication Techniques

Know whom to call when issues arise.

The structure of the project team should be defined so that both your organization and the software vendor understand whom to contact if the project is not proceeding as planned or if any significant issues arise during the course of the project. It is the "escalation path" that details the reporting hierarchy throughout the implementation project. Be sure the software vendor has provided your organization with an escalation path to efficiently address any issues that arise during the implementation.

Working with the Software Vendor

Managing the Project

Your people and company culture will make your implementation unique to all others.

Although a software vendor may have vast experience implementing your new accounting software, each implmentation is unique due to the singular personalities and processes within each organization. Because most software offers several alternatives for completing each specific business task, decisions regarding how the software will be configured must be made based on your organization's business requirements and corporate culture. This culture and the decisions made throughout the implementation will make your accounting software project unique from any other implementation. Understanding this reality will create the proper mind-set and focus among project team members necessary to successfully complete the project.

Working with the Software Vendor

Managing the Project

Your organization is responsible for implementing the new software. The software vendor is there to assist you.

Do not depend on the software vendor to manage your implementation. The vendor's role is to assist. Organizations often place all of the responsibility of project success on the vendor. Your organization's project team, not the software vendor, will be ultimately responsible for the success or failure of the project. The vendor's role is to transfer knowledge of the software to your team and to advise your team during the implementation process. The vendor will most likely be handling several customer implementations simultaneously, but your organization is managing only one project, so take the time to ensure that your implementation project is being managed properly.

Working with the Software Vendor

Managing the Project

Define a way to monitor the progress and success of the project.

The primary goal of a software vendor is to ensure that your organization is satisfied with the purchase of the new software. Beyond that, it is your organization's responsibility to communicate how you will evaluate project performance and success. Clearly define expectations so they can be monitored throughout the project. You should identify specific objectives before beginning the project so that it is very clear to your organization whether or not the implementation project was a success. Examples include: "We will not spend over $100,000 implementing this new software," or "We will be up and running on this new software within nine months," or "Eighty percent of our users will be happy with the performance of the new software." You do not need to share these objectives with all project team members, but the management team should agree on objectives before the project begins.

Chapter 4

Implementation Planning

Defining how you will implement the new software will keep the project on track and ensure that team members understand their roles and responsibilities. The plan must be realistic and should be broken down into smaller projects that will provide many opportunities for success. The focus should be on keeping the project as simple as possible; however, you should expect that the new software implementation will result in personnel and process changes within the organization.

Implementation Planning

Setting Expectations

Good, fast, and cheap. Don't expect all three!

If most executives could have their way, the new software implementation would be done well (good), in a very short time frame (fast), and with little expense (cheap). An old saying is that you can typically expect your project to have only two of these three characteristics (at best!). It may be good and fast, but it won't be cheap. It may be good and cheap, but it won't be fast. It may be cheap and fast, but it won't be good! Select which characteristics are most critical to your organization. With these priorities in mind, build strategies and timelines that meet these goals.

Implementation Planning

Setting Expectations

Be ready to deal with some shortcomings.

Most likely, you have been running on your existing software for several years. Over these years, the software may have been modified and fine-tuned to look and feel exactly as needed. Do not expect the new software to replace all of your existing software's functionality immediately upon implementation. Rather, ensure that "must have" functionality exists immediately and create a plan for dealing with shortcomings at the outset. Identifying shortcomings ahead of time will allow your project team to communicate these issues prior to deployment so that users can be trained on how to work around the shortcomings. Once the initial deployment phase is complete and users are familiar with how to process the required tasks, the shortcomings should be listed and prioritized so that they can be addressed in the proper order. Review this list with your project team to ensure that issues are prioritized properly.

Implementation Planning

Managing the Project

Set aside time specifically for managing the implementation project.

Ten to twenty percent of all time spent by your organization on the software implementation project should relate specifically to managing the project itself. This includes keeping in touch with the software vendor to confirm appointments and training schedules and meeting with the project team regularly to verify that the project is proceeding as expected. This type of work does not directly yield results so it is often overlooked, but organization and communication are the two most important skills in navigating your way through an implementation project. Understanding that these elements require a significant amount of time will set expectations for the staff and project team that this implementation project must be successful. Other administrative tasks that must be done regularly include reviewing the project budget, meeting with upper management to communicate the status of the project, and confirming the status of all planned and in-progress tasks.

Implementation Planning

Managing the Project

Create a plan before you begin the project.

Prior to beginning the actual implementation steps, verify that your team clearly understands the process that will be used to implement the new software. Specifically, if the vendor is assisting with the implementation, you should require that the vendor demonstrate to you a proven implementation methodology prior to beginning the implementation. Alternatively, if you plan to handle the majority of the implementation internally, document the plan for how you will be transitioning from your current software to the new software. This methodology can be a high-level document, but it should include a timeline so that it is clear how much time will be available for the completion of each task. At a minimum, the document should detail the due dates for completing key project tasks and milestones. A milestone is a key event in a project that typically has an impact on the entire project timeline if the event has to be rescheduled, so it is important to meet these milestone event dates to keep the project on schedule.

Implementation Planning

Managing the Project

Begin the project with a formal kickoff meeting.

Always begin any new project with a formal kickoff meeting. Invite all team members and clearly communicate the goals and objectives of the new software implementation. Be open and honest regarding expectations during the implementation period, and be sure to ask each individual to voice any concerns they may have related to the project. A great way to obtain an honest response is to have each team member submit an anonymous list of questions, issues, and concerns to the project sponsor prior to or after the kickoff meeting. This strategy will avoid any potentially uncomfortable scenarios for the team members and will make each team member feel that his or her opinions are respected and valued.

Implementation Planning

Managing the Project

A project charter is a document that defines the project.

A primary element of the project kickoff meeting is the creation of a project charter document. This document defines the scope of the project, the project team members, a timeline, a budget, and other implementation expectations. The project scope defines what will be included in the project. It is also a good idea to document what will *not* be included in the project to avoid any errors of omission. The project charter also serves as a formal way to communicate the planned steps of the project to the project team. This document does not have to detail the project's individual tasks, but it should be used as a reference for guiding the overall direction of the project. Finally, each team member's role and responsibilities should be outlined as part of the project charter so that everyone is aware of each team member's duties throughout the project.

Implementation Planning

Managing the Project

Small project tasks result in many successful mini-projects.

It is very common to become overwhelmed by the amount of work that must be done to complete the implementation of new software. At the beginning of the project, it is not uncommon for the team to feel that the software will never get implemented due to the amount of work ahead. To avoid this perception and simultaneously generate confidence and a positive outlook, divide the implementation into a series of small projects and tasks that are less daunting and have a greater likelihood of being successfully accomplished. Break the tasks down so that no single task takes longer that one or two days. Some natural tasks may need to be artificially segemented into sub-tasks in order to meet this two-day limit. For example, if it will take five days to enter all vendors into the new software, create tasks that include vendors A-G, H-M, and N-Z so that each task is approximately one to two days. To acknowledge the efforts of the project team, be sure to formally recognize each completed task during a weekly project status meeting.

Implementation Planning

Managing the Project

Focus the priorities on the daily business tasks.

When prioritizing the implementation objectives, focus on the areas that are essential to running your day-to-day business. For example, let's assume that two current priorities within your implementation project are to integrate the human resources (HR) module and provide for electronic payment processing within the new software. If any re-prioritization is needed at any point in the project to ensure that the project stays on schedule, these two priorities can be easily de-prioritized. The HR module can be de-prioritized because it benefits a small percentage of the total user community. The electronic payment processing feature may also be de-prioritized because it is completed infrequently or randomly. Be sure that the focus of the project is on the areas that affect the largest number of users on a regular basis. This methodology will not only provide the greatest return on investment, but it will also garner the greatest buy-in from the project team as more team members will benefit directly from the key objectives of the project.

Implementation Planning

Managing the Project

Use an escalation path to formalize the chain of command during the project.

Once the project team is defined, formally communicate the escalation path that will be used to address any issues that arise during the implementation project. The escalation path clearly defines the individual to whom each person reports during the project. A typical escalation path may be that the end user reports issues to a designated project team member. The team member either resolves the issue or reports the issue to the project manager. If the project manager is unable to resolve the issue, it is reported to the executive sponsor of the project. At this point, either a decision is made or the project team should meet as a group to discuss the issue and vote on a proposed resolution.

Implementation Planning

Managing the Project

Let the entire project team know that the escalation of project issues to the management team is a good thing.

Initially, the escalation plan will be viewed negatively by the project team, and team members may attempt to hide issues or errors in order to avoid having an issue escalated to the management team. To avoid this perception, explicitly state to each team member that management realizes that implementation of new software is not a regular event and escalation of issues is expected. Also, make it clear that team members should not be offended or upset by such escalations. Rather, the most important element of escalation is resolving the issue in a timely manner. Once an issue is escalated, it is important that it be resolved as soon as possible to avoid any disruption of the project schedule or budget. Project team members should be complimented when they escalate issues, as these efforts help to keep the project on track.

Implementation Planning

Managing the Project

Hold a weekly project status meeting.

The two primary purposes of a regularly scheduled project meeting are to review the status of the project and to create a forum for asking questions and voicing concerns. Warning: an unwillingness to dedicate one hour per week to a project status meeting is a clear indication of limited commitment to the project. A great way to organize the meeting is to divide the meeting into three specific segments. The first segment is: "What did we do last week?" This segment serves as a great motivational tool by praising the most recent accomplishments of the team. The second segment is: "What are we doing this week?" This segment reviews the current open tasks and reminds the team members that they are expected to complete specific tasks by the end of the week. The third segment is: "What will we be doing next week?" This segment provides a planning tool for future tasks and sets the expectations for what is to be accomplished in the short-term future. Prior to adjourning the meeting, ask formally if there are any other topics or concerns that should be discussed. Utilize this formula to proactively manage the project and stay current on the progress of each task.

Implementation Planning

Managing the Project

Create a project change form to track changes to the original implementation plan.

One of the most frequent reasons for project failure is a lack of control on changes to the plan after the implementation has begun. Changes should be expected throughout any software implementation project, but without formally documenting each change and analyzing its impact on the project, decisions may be made that are detrimental to the success of the project. To address this concern, define a formal document and procedure for managing changes to the implementation plan. This document should include sections that define the description of the change, which users are impacted, the anticipated impact on the project budget and timeline, and an alternative proposal that may avoid the need for the proposed change. The project team should review these changes collectively so that the group can make an informed decision as to which changes should be accepted or rejected.

Implementation Planning

Managing the Project

Create a way to measure success at the end of the project.

It is often very difficult to accurately gauge the overall success of a software implementation because there are so many intangible elements that can factor into the equation. The best way to analyze the success of the project is to define at least five to ten specific objectives that the organization hopes to achieve as a result of implementing the new software. To provide an even better scoring system, prioritize each of the objectives to ensure that the project team maintains focus on the most significant objectives of the project. The objectives list will also provide the project team with a clear vision of why the organization is going through the effort and expense of implementing the new software.

Implementation Planning

Defining the Project Scope

Know what features and objectives will NOT be included in the project.

"Project scope" is a term that is commonly used to refer to the elements that will be included within any project. As part of the planning phase, clearly define the scope of the project by explicitly stating what will and will not be included in the project. Listing what will not be included is just as important as listing what will be included, as the "not included" list will eliminate any incorrect assumptions and misinterpretations by project team members as to what will not be included within the project.

Implementation Planning

Defining the Project Scope

The project is not over when you begin using the new software.

Plan for the implementation project to have at least two phases. Because of the specific nature of accounting software, some processes and functions should not be implemented until after all users have begun processing transactions. For example, a custom-integrated Web site cannot be successfully launched until the back-office order processing and accounting modules have been fully implemented and all customers and items have been defined in the new software. The first phase of the implementation should focus on all required funtionality, while the second phase of the project should focus on any non-required functionality. In addition, the follow-up phases of the project can include any new requirements that are discovered during the course of the project, so that the project timeline is not disrupted. Even if there are no secondary phases of the project, the project should not be considered finished until each individual business process or transaction has been completed at least once in the new software.

Implementation Planning

Defining the Project Scope

Follow-up project phases are faster, easier—and happier—to complete.

While the first phase of a software implementation must include all functions that are essential to running the day-to-day business, planning for follow-up phases within the implementation project will ease the burden on the project team during the first phase of the project. In addition, follow-up phases typically have a much higher success factor than phase one tasks because users are already familiar with the new software and will learn any additional processes or functions much quicker than during the initial deployment of the software.

Implementation Planning

Project Team Responsibilities

The executive sponsor is responsible for oversight of the project.

Identify the executive sponsor of the project. This individual has oversight of the project tasks and budget and is the highest level of the escalation path. This person does not need detailed knowledge of how the software works, but this individual should have a good understanding of the organization along with full decision-making authority in order to serve as arbitor during project team debates and assist with making key business and software decisions. At a minimum, the executive sponsor should attend the weekly project status meeting so that the team can see that management is committed to the project's success.

Implementation Planning

Project Team Responsibilities

A project manager manages the day-to-day tasks of the project.

The internal project manager must have excellent organizational skills and a solid understanding of the organization's processes, staff capabilities, and objectives of the implementation. This individual does not need to understand the intricate details of every process, but must be able to coordinate the required resources over the course of the project to ensure that all key processes have been represented during the training phase of the implementation. A typical mid-market accounting software implementation typically takes approximately four to six months to complete from kickoff through the first month-end close. With this timeline, the project manager should expect to spend approximately twenty-five to fifty percent of his or her time on the project. The shorter the implementation timeline, the higher percentage the project manager will need to dedicate to the project. In order to cope with such a workload shift, consider reassigning some of the project manager's day-to-day tasks to other staff members until the project is completed.

Implementation Planning

Project Team Responsibilities

Your project manager should ALWAYS be the individual who can most successfully lead your software implementation project.

Implementing new software is one of the most significant projects that any organization will undertake. Thus, when selecting the project manager, it is very important to select the most capable candidate for this role, despite his or her existing responsibilities. In most organizations, the most ideal candidate's workload is already too high and this candidate will not have the necessary time to devote to this project. Do not consider an already high current workload as a deterrent for selecting this individual to lead your project. Instead, review the candidate's current workload and temporarily reassign some of the tasks to other individuals so that the candidate can give the proper amount of attention and focus to this new project, with the understanding that tasks will be returned once the implementation has been completed.

Implementation Planning

Project Team Responsibilities

Create a diverse project team so that all key business areas are represented.

Because most organizations have many interrelated roles and responsibilities, every business process must be respresented by at least one individual on the project team. In smaller organizations, it is common to have one individual who represents multiple business processes or roles, whereas in larger organizations, there may be multiple individuals who represent each key business process or role. The risk in not having every process represented on the project team is that a key element of an existing business process might not be considered because the existing project team members were not aware of it. It is always better to begin with a large project team and dismiss team members than to start with too few members and then have to figure out who should be included after the project has started, since this would require the new individual to play "catch-up" to be able to contribute as needed.

Implementation Planning

Project Team Responsibilities

Be prepared to revise your employees' job titles, roles, and responsibilities when the new software is deployed.

The differences between your current software and the new software may result in changes to existing employees' roles and responsibilities. Be prepared to revise job titles, roles, and responsibilities as necessary. Typically, as technology advances, many of the time-consuming processes that staff members performed manually are replaced by automated or more efficient processes provided by the software. Most employees will still be required to efficiently run the business, but they will now be able to serve in positions that add more value to the organization. For example, assume that the new software provides for electronic customer order submission or for real-time customer order entry by the sales representative. Rather than this gain in efficiency resulting in a lost job for an existing staff member, the employee will have time to review orders for accuracy, follow up on customer quotes, call customers when an order is to be shipped late, and advise customers of upcoming product promotions. All of these tasks clearly provide more value to the organization than the manual typing of customer orders into the former software.

Implementation Planning

Project Team Responsibilities

For each task to be completed, formally define who is responsible and the date by which the task is to be completed.

Breaking the project down into manageable tasks will significantly improve your project team's morale. However, for each task to be completed, you must formally define who is responsible and the date by which the task is to be completed. It is human nature to procrastinate those things that are most uncomfortable, and since most people are not comfortable with the types of tasks assigned during the (infrequent) implementation of new software, these tasks tend to be put off the most. The formal tracking of responsibilities communicates to the project team that each team member will be accountable for completing assigned tasks in a timely manner.

Implementation Planning

Managing Risk

Keep the project simple by limiting the introduction of new processes in the initial deployment.

While the organization may be excited to begin using the new software in order to leverage all of its great features, it is important not to overload the staff with new processes and functions during the initial deployment. The primary focus of the project team should be adapting current business processes to the new software. Limiting the number of new features utilized will provide users with the time required to focus on learning how to process existing business transactions in the new software. The other reason to limit any new functions is to avoid the perception that the new software is more cumbersome and difficult to use than the existing software. It is very common for users to simply declare that the new software is more difficult to work with instead of appreciating the additional benefits and reasons behind why an extra step or two may be required to complete a transaction. Once users are comfortable working with the software and their confidence has improved, begin introducing new features and functions based on a prioritized list that details the order in which new features are to be introduced.

Implementation Planning

Managing Risk

To ensure the success of the initial implementation, eliminate all project objectives that carry significant risk.

Within each business process, there will be many opportunities for process improvement. Each opportunity should be evaluated carefully and implemented only if the opportunity presents little or no risk to the success of the initial deployment. A primary way to achieve this is by implementing the software using your current business processes and then rolling out revised and enhanced processes after users have become comfortable. As an example, if the purchasing system utilized today consists of inventory reports and the manual creation of purchase orders but the new software provides an automated purchasing system, consider continuing the manual purchasing method until after the users have become familiar with the steps required to complete the manual process before introducing the automated system. Later, the automated system can be slowly rolled out to the user community by selecting a subset of vendors or items to automate. This method results in a strong foundation of understanding how the software works as well as a much lower risk of problems and issues during the deployment process. Apply this methodology to all areas of the new software.

Implementation Planning

Managing Risk

Take the time to evaluate all project risks honestly.

There are inherent risks in implementing any new software package. All project risks must be honestly assessed prior to beginning the project so that these risks can be evaluated and addressed as appropriate. Honestly assessing these risks will increase the likelihood of project success. Masking or failing to acknowledge existing risks will only delay the negative consequences after the project has started. Typical risks that should be considered include the seasonality of the business, the loss of a key employee, extended vacations or leaves of absence, relocation of the business, unavailabilty of resources due to existing workloads, or the acquisition or sale of another company or business unit. The key to dealing with risk is to acknowledge it and plan accordingly to minimize the impact each risk presents.

Implementation Planning

Managing Risk

Make the project team aware of all project risks to improve the odds of success.

Once the project risks have been defined, it is important to share concerns about these risks with the entire project team. By sharing this information with the entire team, you are letting all team members know that their own concerns are valid and they will be addressed accordingly. Sharing information also provides a forum for obtaining input and recommendations from the team on how to best deal with these risks. Finally, team members may point out other risks or issues that have not been mentioned previously.

Implementation Planning

Selecting a Deployment Date

Pick a planned deployment date that is attainable yet provides a sense of urgency.

Your planned deployment date for the new software should be a date that is attainable yet still conveys a sense of urgency. Scheduling an early deployment date that seems unattainable will increase the stress levels of the project team and will most likely result in feelings of failure and frustration as the date is inevitably not met. An overly aggressive deployment date may also reduce the quality of the work since the project team will be rushing through assignments in order to complete them by the due date. Conversely, scheduling a date too far into the future will not allow the project to gain the momentum required to keep the team focused. Select a date that everyone agrees is attainable so that the entire team can be part of this crucial decision.

Implementation Planning

Selecting a Deployment Date

Use a visual timeline to determine how much time is required to complete the implementation.

Too many people mistakenly believe that new software can be implemented in a matter of weeks. The actuality is that it will take four to six months to implement most software packages. The timeframe will be longer than expected because team members will not be able to focus all of their time on the project. Instead, the implementation project is a new task that has been added to their existing responsibilities. Also, "delays" frequently occur because organizations will use the implementation of new software as a time to review all current business processes in an effort to document or improve the existing procedures. To determine your expected deployment date, list all of the activities that need to take place during the implementation and then begin working backward from a tentative deployment date to the current date to see if enough time is available to complete the implementation at a comfortable pace. This plan should include at least two additional weeks to account for delays due to unforeseen events.

Chapter 5

Software Design

Many software packages provide the ability to customize them. Some packages allow you to modify only documents and reports, while others provide tools for changing the underlying business logic to meet your organization's needs. For packages with modifiable business logic, there are no limits as to how you can use the software. However, you must take care to ensure that the modifications are required and have been designed and completed properly.

Software Design

Defining Software Requirements

Modify the software only when absolutely necessary.

The only time a modification to the new software is warranted *during the implementation project* is when the standard software prevents you from completing a required task. This guideline is critical to managing the implementation budget and timeline. In cases when you cannot complete a key task without modification, attempt to use a temporary work-around to accomplish the task until users can become more familiar with the software. Once users become familiar with the software through daily use, they may realize that the existing method is actually not as difficult as it initially appeared and no modifications are then necessary. If you find that you require a modification to the software after initial use, any existing off-line processing or work-around solutions can be eliminated when the modifications are complete.

Software Design

Defining Software Requirements

Don't be afraid to ask why.

The implementation of new software is an excellent opportunity to ask why. While reviewing how each process is handled within your organization, ask "why" in an effort to find ways to reduce the number of steps required to complete the transaction. A common mistake made during an implementation project is forcing the new software to perform tasks that should be eliminated due to outdated business rules or organizational practices that are no longer valuable. Attempting to utilize the new software as-is may result in a more efficient business process without having to make any modifications to the software.

Software Design

Defining Software Requirements

Maintain a gap list throughout the initial training of the project team.

As your project team becomes familiar with the new software, create and maintain a "gap list" that documents all discrepancies between the functionality of the software and your organization's requirements. Do not act to resolve any of these gaps until after the entire initial user training phase has been completed. This ensures that one area of the software does not receive more attention than other areas simply because they were the first to be covered during user training. Waiting until all training is complete allows the project team to review all gaps as a whole and fairly prioritize the list according to which gaps have the greatest impact on day-to-day operations. Additionally, after all areas of the software have been reviewed, the project team may find that many items on the list are not relevant and should be removed. Focus on resolving the gaps that have the greatest impact on the organization. To determine impact, consider the number of users affected by the gap, the frequency of the transaction, and the overall relevance of the gap.

Software Design

Defining Software Requirements

Use a "specification" document to formalize any modifications to the new software.

Each change to the new software should be formally documented on an enhancement specification (spec) document. The project manager and the executive sponsor should both sign this document prior to beginning the development of the modification. Not only does this document provide short-term benefits by giving a detailed explanation of the modification, it can also serve as a testing guide, a user documentation guide, and a post-implementation reference guide for users who may not recall the detailed design of a custom feature. Ideally, this document should include a description of the changes to be made, as well as a section to define the existing functionality of the software or other work-around solutions available if the enhancement is not completed. This will allow the decision makers to make a more informed decision about whether the modification is necessary.

Software Design

Testing the Software

Test the software thoroughly to ensure accurate processing and reporting.

While the software vendor will test each change made to the software and will assist your project team with defining business processes and workflows, it is the responsibility of your organization to test and accept the effectiveness of all modifications made. This guideline is not intended to deflect responsibility from the vendor, rather it is required because your project team will undoubtedly be more familiar with your organization's requirements than the vendor ever could be. Ultimately, the project team must ensure that all critical business processes are functioning properly. The optimal approach is to thoroughly test and formally accept each modification to the software within thirty days to avoid delays in the project.

Chapter 6

Training

The two types of training that occur during an implementation project are project team training and end-user training. The project team must receive training on the basic functionality of the new software. This training is ongoing throughout the project, whereas the training of the end users does not need to occur until the actual deployment date approaches. Provide documentation and support to all end users to facilitate a smooth transition to the new software.

Training

Training the Project Team

The software vendor's #1 job is to transfer knowledge of the software to your organization.

The primary responsibility of the software vendor is to transfer knowledge of how the new software functions to your project team. Your project team is responsible for the overall success of the implementation. This fact should be explicitly stated to the project team so that team members are aware of their responsibilities. Also, explain to team members that they should utilize the vendor whenever necessary to answer any questions instead of making assumptions or delaying the project. Gathering a list of questions or issues and presenting them to the vendor at the same time (such as the weekly project status meeting) will make the best use of time and will allow the entire team to hear the information provided by the vendor.

Training

Training the Project Team

Learn how the software works.

First, learn how the software works. Next, learn how the software works. Finally, learn how the software works. If you do not do these three things prior to deploying the software, you are significantly increasing the risk that the software will not accomplish the expected result. Most likely you will also exceed the project budget due to being overly dependent on the software vendor to assist your organization with running the software in the initial weeks and months after the software is deployed. Deployment is the phase of the implementation when most organizations exceed the budget. Many implementations will progress on time and on budget until deployment; however, at that point, you will quickly find out if the project team and other users indeed took the time to learn how the software works. To avoid this scenario, require each project team member to demonstrate how each process is completed in the new software. In addition to demonstrating each team member's knowledge of the new software, this also provides an excellent way to cross train the project team on other areas of the software.

Training

Training the Project Team

The project team should train the other users of the software.

While it is common for the software vendor to conduct the end-user training, the ideal scenario is to have your project team lead the end-user training sessions. End-user training performed by project team members signals that the key members of your organization understand the software and are comfortable with supporting the other users. A more tangible benefit of this training approach is that end users will be able to go to team members for help during software deployment, thereby controlling the overall budget by reducing short-term and long-term dependence on the vendor.

Training

Training the Project Team

The project manager should attend all training sessions.

To ensure that your project manager is able to effectively manage the project, this individual should attend or monitor all training sessions. While this individual does not need to understand the intricate details of each business process, he or she must understand how each business process impacts other areas of the organization and the software implementation. Because it is common for transactions to flow from one module to the next within accounting software, it is critical that at least one individual be aware of what is discussed within each training session so that each type of transaction flows smoothly from one module to the next. In addition to workflow decisions, there are typically areas of training that overlap from one user group to the next. For example, both the sales team and the credit and collections departments may need to know how to review a customer's account balance. By attending both training sessions, the project manager will be able to confirm that the training occurs consistantly across departments.

Training

End-User Training

End-user training should occur approximately three to four weeks before the deployment date.

Training the end users three to four weeks prior to the deployment date provides the users with the best chance of a successful deployment. End-user training sessions held more than four weeks prior to deployment will result in retraining when the deployment date finally arrives. Conversely, training the end users less than three weeks prior to the deployment will make the end users feel that they did not receive enough time to train on the new software. By training three to four weeks prior to deployment, users have enough time to digest all of the training material and adequate time to practice what was learned without feeling as if their training was rushed or incomplete.

Training

End-User Training

Don't rely on a standard software user manual for training your users.

Standard software user manuals are a good reference for becoming familiar with new software. However, each organization is unique, and these standard user guides do not consider your organization's unique qualities. Custom end-user training documentation should be created for all significant business processes so that your organization's specific requirements can be included. Investing the time and energy to create custom training guides will not only reduce the amount of time needed to train your end users, but it will also serve as a guide for training new employees on your business processes. Lastly, documenting the procedures to be followed by the end users will serve as another way to ensure that each process has been thoroughly tested in the new software. These custom training guides should be continually updated after the implementation of the new software as your business processes develop over time.

Training

End-User Training

Think of the software vendor as a coach during end-user training.

During end-user training, have the software vendor available to ensure that the end-user training performed by the project team is accurate and complete. Having the vendor available will also serve as backup or support in case a training session led by a project team member is not going as planned. If the vendor cannot be present or the budget is not available, then prior to end-user training, arrange for the vendor to meet with each project team member to review the end-user training plan and to coach the team on how to best complete the required sessions so that maximum benefit is achieved at each one.

Training

End-User Training

Hand out a training guide for each user training session.

All end-user training documentation should be completed prior to beginning any end-user training session. Every training session should include a custom user training guide for the project team to guide the users through the process. This documentation should also be used by the end users after the session has been completed for continued training and throughout deployment. For a typical user, it is very easy to follow along with a professional trainer as the material is reviewed in a classroom environment, but once the users return to their workstations, they become immediately lost and frustrated if they have not received specific instructions on how to begin and complete a transaction. A one- to four-page document highlighting the key steps of each process will go a long way toward improving user satisfaction and minimizing the financial impact of deploying the software by limiting your organization's dependence on the vendor. In most cases, the software vendor will welcome the smooth deployment as a sign of a successful project and a happy customer.

Training

End-User Training

Provide a "playground" for users to practice what they learned in the user training sessions.

Between end-user training and the deployment date, end users should utilize a training database to practice lessons learned during the training sessions. Practicing what was learned will sharpen their skills prior to deployment, resulting in reduced stress levels during deployment. Practicing on the software may also bring up issues or questions that were not previously known to the project team. Uncovering these issues prior to deployment provides the opportunity to resolve the issues before they affect live transactions. If the issues are signficant, the deployment can be postponed if necessary, which is always better than finding these issues after you have already deployed the new software. If project team members have fullfilled their responsibilities throughout the project, most issues found by end users during practice sessions will be minor and quickly resolvable.

Training

End-User Training

Utilize technology to lower the cost of training.

Technology continues to play an increasingly significant role throughout the global business community. While there are certainly industries that have taken greater advantage of the latest technologies, software training is one area where every business can benefit. There are many Internet-based training and teleconferencing services available that allow trainers to share their computer desktop with groups of other users—ideal for a software implementation project. These services often provide a telephone number so that all members can listen in as the presenter navigates through the software via the Internet. Internet-based training is a great tool for minimizing travel expenses associated with implementing software. Also, without having to consider travel expenses or travel time, Internet-based training allows your organization to break the training into much shorter sessions, enabling users to retain a higher percentage of the material covered while also resulting in a reduced disruption to their regular schedules. Despite the advantages to Internet-based training, on-site training conducted by the vendor should be used for any extensive or complex training sessions. For user training beyond the implementation, utilize a screen capture tool that is capable of capturing audio and generating video files. These files can be saved and made available to users electronically via a network, e-mail, or Intranet. These files can be used for several purposes including: electronically "documenting" a business process, training new users on the software, and rolling out new features to the existing user community.

Chapter 7

Data Conversion

Unless your organization is a new business that is not transitioning from another software package, you will need to convert data into the new software. This data conversion process can be a major task and can derail even the best implementation plans. Attempt to manually enter as much data as possible into the new software and thoroughly review all converted data prior to deployment.

Data Conversion

Planning and Data Mapping

Manually convert as much data as possible.

The automated conversion of data from the existing software to the new software is not a shortcut to a faster and easier implementation. Plan on manually converting as much data as possible. Manual entry of data into the new software is an excellent opportunity to "clean up" the existing data by eliminating obsolete or irrelevant data. Reentry of data is also an excellent opportunity to update the existing data and remedy any incomplete or inaccurate data prior to deployment of the new software. Lastly, due to differences between how the existing software and the new software store data, manual data entry also enables your organization to recode the data to a format that is most suitable for use in the new software.

Data Conversion

Planning and Data Mapping

Manual input of data is the best possible training method.

Aside from the many other benefits of manually entering your data into the new software, manual conversion of data (such as customers, vendors, and orders) most importantly provides an excellent way to familiarize the users with the software. It allows the user community to feel a sense of ownership of the new software even before deployment or end-user training. Through manual entry of data, users become familiar with navigating through the software, experience how to enter and find data, and learn where specific data is stored. Consider an organization that has 2,000 customers. By having five individuals split the entry of all customers over eight weeks, each user is required to enter only ten customers into the new software per day. The repetition of entering hundreds of customers over several weeks is an excellent training tool.

Data Conversion

Planning and Data Mapping

Automated conversion should be used only for files containing more than 1,000 records.

If you have fewer than 1,000 records in a file or table, manually input these records into the new software. For all of the various reasons already listed (good training, data cleanup, data ownership), manual data entry is an excellent way to get the project off to a strong start. As long as there are fewer than 1,000 records, any inefficiencies experienced in the time required to manually input data is more than made up for by the benefits received.

Data Conversion

Planning and Data Mapping

For worst-case implementation scenarios, utilize the "enter as you go" option.

Despite everything that is already known about data conversion planning, testing, and execution, there are times when organizations are not afforded the opportunity to follow a conservative approach to getting the data into the new software. This may be due to a very aggressive timeline or because resources are simply not available to complete the project using best practices. In these cases, a final option is to simply deploy the software and enter data as transactions need to be completed in the new software. For example, if your organization does not have the time to enter or convert all of the vendors into the new software, verify that all of the defaults and setups have been defined properly before deployment and then enter each vendor into the system as the first purchase order or invoice is executed. This option certainly will require additional time per transaction over the initial weeks and months on the new software, but it will also provide the highest level of assurance that the data that does exist is the most up-to-date and relevant data possible. As already mentioned, this is an aggressive approach that implies no testing of the software prior to deployment and should be utilized only as a last resort.

Data Conversion

Testing the Converted Data

Electronically converted data must be reviewed and edited record by record.

Even when using an automated electronic data conversion tool, plan on having the project team spend a significant amount of time reviewing and editing the converted data in the new software. This manual review and editing of data is required because there are typically fields that exist in the prior software that do not exist in the new software and cannot be automatically converted, and vice versa. These discrepancies may require the user to manually input a value to each of these fields. Finally, the detailed review of the converted data is an excellent opportunity to clean and reformat the data prior to deployment. Having clean data that can be trusted by the user community will be a welcome improvement as the new software is deployed.

Data Conversion

Testing the Converted Data

Run at least one test of the data conversion programs prior to deployment.

If using automated electronic data conversion tools, perform at least one full data conversion test prior to the final deployment. Run this test in a separate testing environment so that the data can be adjusted and reconverted if it is found to be inaccurate or incomplete. This test should also assist with defining the total amount of time required to run all data conversion programs, useful for planning the logistics of the cutover from the existing software to the new software. Lastly, this test will provide an opportunity for the user community to review the data for accuracy prior to converting the data in the live environment.

Data Conversion

Testing the Converted Data

Your project team members must confirm the accuracy of data converted into the new software.

Confirming the accuracy of data converted into the new software is the responsibility of the project team. While the software vendor can be responsible for executing the data conversion programs, the vendor should not be assigned to review the data and "approve" it. The software vendor cannot be expected to understand your unique data requirements or what meaningful data may be missing from the new software. Verify that the appropriate project team members understand that they are responsible for reviewing the converted data. Specifically, for each data file that is converted, verify that at least one project team member has confirmed that all data is present, accurate, and in the proper location. In addition to users confirming that the data has been accurately converted, they should also confirm that the expected results are carried through to the general ledger and that all required reports can be generated using the converted data. These tests are critical for confirming that the data has been converted to the proper fields in the new software.

Data Conversion

Executing the Final Data Conversion

Begin converting data into the new software at least one week prior to deployment.

At least one week prior to the deployment date, the final conversions of static data should be completed. This includes all non-transactional data (i.e., customers, vendors, items) and all related data (such as comments, prices, costs, or other related information). This plan will provide enough time to review the converted data prior to beginning the processing of live transactions in the new software and will provide a window of time to allow for the entry of open sales orders, purchase orders, or production orders prior to the deployment date. In essence, this method creates a "pre-deployment" phase and spreads the deployment tasks and initial use of the software over a longer period of time, which helps ensure that the software is complete and accurate once the cutover date officially arrives.

Data Conversion

Executing the Final Data Conversion

Open sales orders and purchase orders can be entered prior to the deployment date.

Very often, it is known that some sales orders, purchase orders, and production orders will not be completed prior to the deployment date of the new software. In that case, these documents should be entered into the new software before the deployment date. Only open quantities should be converted into the new software since previous shipments, receipts, and production output cannot generally be converted on an order-by-order basis. The benefit of completing these tasks prior to the deployment date is that users can be performing tasks in the new software several days or even weeks prior to the cutover date. The experience of completing these tasks in advance will ease the transition to the new software. In order to execute this plan, all customers, vendors, items, and other related information must exist in the new software prior to the entry of orders. In most implementations, the customer, vendor, and item files should be converted at least one or two weeks in advance of the deployment date in order to troubleshoot any data issues.

Data Conversion

Executing the Final Data Conversion

Tracking of purchase orders received but not invoiced requires special attention.

One of the finer points of an accounting software implementation for product-oriented organizations is how to handle purchase orders for products that have been received into inventory but have not yet been invoiced as of the cutover date. This is only a concern if: (1) the existing accounting software allowed the receipt of a purchase order without a vendor invoice, and (2) the software completed an entry to the general ledger to record the increase to inventory and liability for the expected amount of the goods received. When this situation occurs, the staff must manually track which purchase orders have been received but not invoiced in the existing accounting software as of the cutover date to the new software. To track these open purchase orders, a spreadsheet should be created containing the purchase order number, vendor, and dollar amount received but not invoiced. Then, as the vendor invoices arrive, the user will directly debit the liability account that was credited in the existing software during the receipt of the goods. The staff will continue to mark the purchase orders as "invoiced" until all vendor invoices have been received. This same method may be required for customer return orders and vendor return orders if similar functionality existed in the existing software.

Data Conversion

Executing the Final Data Conversion

Conversion of on-hand inventory requires tight controls on inventory-related activities during the cutover to the new software.

For organizations that inventory product, in order to convert on-hand inventory accurately to the new software, all activities must be coordinated to ensure that the reconciliation of inventory can be completed accurately. Specifically, define a cutoff time and communicate to all users which inventory-related transactions should be completed in the existing software prior to that time. Next, perform some level of physical inventory review, import the on-hand quantities into the new software, and reconcile the beginning inventory in the new software to the ending inventory in the existing software. The ultimate goal is to have as few "mid-process" transactions as possible as of the cutoff point. Prior to the cutoff, make sure that all shipped sales orders have been invoiced. Also, make sure that all pending inventory adjustments, returns, and purchase order receipts are clearly documented so that they can be referenced in the future.

Data Conversion

Executing the Final Data Conversion

Converting A/R and A/P balances should be done after they have been reconciled in the existing software.

Similar to on-hand inventory, open payable and open receivable balances should be converted as soon as possible, but only after a cutoff point in the existing accounting software. Depending on its capabilities, it may be an option to begin using the new software prior to converting open payables and receivables. This would allow users to complete all activities from last month and fully reconcile to the general ledger prior to converting these files. Regardless of the capabilities of the new software, these files should be converted as soon as possible to avoid data reconciliation issues. The likelihood of reconciliation issues increases as time passes between the cutover date and the conversion of the open records into the new software.

Chapter 8

Deployment

The decision to "go live" and deploy the new software formally kicks off the deployment process. This process should begin several weeks prior to the official cutover and continue through the first month-end close on the new software. Establish a well-documented plan to ensure consideration of all aspects of the deployment as the cutover occurs. A formal meeting to end the project provides a sense of accomplishment to the project team and keeps the momentum going by setting the priorities for future goals related to how the organization will use the new software.

Deployment

Preparing for Deployment

The go-live decision is the most important day of the project.

The go-live decision (deciding the date when the new software will "go live") puts into motion a series of events that will prepare the organization for deploying the new software. These events include: end-user training, final data conversion, document/form ordering and testing, and planning the logistics of the cutover to the new software. In order to allow for all of these events to occur comfortably, you should make the go-live decision at least thirty days prior to the actual cutover date. On the go-live decision date, all members of the project team must be confident that all transactions can be completed in the new software. In addition, everyone must agree that all data conversion routines and user documentation aspects have been reviewed and completed as planned. It is common for minor issues to remain, but all major elements of the implementation should be completed as of this milestone date. An easy way to determine if the organization is prepared to deploy in thirty days is by asking, "If the software had to be deployed today, would we be able to effectively run the business?" If the answer to this question is no, then consider postponing the deployment. Delay the deployment if all members of the project team are not in agreement to move forward or if everyone's concerns cannot be addressed.

Deployment

Preparing for Deployment

Create a "go-live checklist" to manage the cutover to the new software.

At least thirty days prior to the deployment date, complete a "go-live checklist" that details the logistics of how and when each deployment step will be completed during the cutover to the new software. This list will signficantly reduce the team's stress levels and will add confidence during the deployment as team members see that the cutover has been carefully planned and will be executed according to a predetermined timeline. Include as much detail as possible on this list and have all project team members review it to recommend additions and to confirm their involvement in the process. Verify that all users understand their responsibilities during this critical timeframe and acknowledge when their tasks will be completed.

Deployment

Preparing for Deployment

Create a "go-live contingency plan" to remedy a worst-case scenario during the transition to the new software.

Converting from the existing software to the new software over a weekend provides an acceptable buffer to resolve any issues that arise during the data transition. Ideally, all activity on the existing software should be cut off at 3:00 p.m. on Friday to allow for adequate time to execute the data transition. A weekend transition also minimizes the amount of "downtime" for end users so that when they arrive on Monday morning, they can immediately begin using the new software. Despite the most careful transition planning by means of a "go-live checklist," a "go-live contingency plan" should also be in place that details the steps to be taken if the software is not ready on Monday morning or if for any reason the deployment of the new software must be postponed until a later date. By having a plan in place beforehand and understanding the consequences of having to postpone the deployment, users will be aware of what is at stake and what all of the options are as the transition weekend takes place.

Deployment

Transitioning to the New Software

Running parallel on two software packages for more than one week will exhaust your staff and will delay the resolution of open issues.

A full parallel testing period involves completing every single transaction in both the existing and new accounting software and then comparing the results of the two packages to ensure consistency. In addition to the obvious hardships placed upon your staff to complete such a test, there are also going to be differences in how each software is used that will naturally lead to different results. Also, users very often do not fully understand the consequences of not completing a transaction in the new software and will often "skip" entering the transaction when they encounter an issue or error because they need to move on and do not have the time to report or resolve the issue. Only if you have a low-volume, high-dollar-value transaction business can you afford to run parallel for more than one week.

Deployment

Transitioning to the New Software

After end-user training, have all users execute every fifth transaction in the new software as they continue to process in the existing software.

Running two accounting systems in parallel for one month is common, but is very difficult on all users. It can be a hindrance to learning the new software because adequate time cannot be allocated to processing transactions in the new software due to the need for duplicate processing. Instead of running both the existing accounting software and the new software in parallel, consider a "mini-parallel" project. Immediately after end-user training, create a training environment that will closely mirror the eventual production software environment. In this training environment, have users perform a random sample of transactions, such as every fifth transaction, over a period of several days. This mini-parallel testing provides practice for the users after training and confirms that each type of daily transaction can be completed as expected in the new software.

Deployment

Transitioning to the New Software

Review printed documents and forms in the new software at least two weeks prior to deployment.

A great initial test of whether the new software is ready to be deployed is to print some of the common documents that will be generated by the new software, such as sales quotes, sales invoices, and purchase orders. If all of the expected information is present and is printing in the expected location, it is a good indicator that the software is ready to be deployed. Before making the go-live decision or very shortly thereafter, verify that all document forms and letterhead that will be used to print forms and documents have been ordered. This will provide adequate time to test the printing of each document on its related form. During testing, print several tests of each document to ensure that the data is printing correctly. Documents to review include purchase quotes, purchase orders, production orders, AP checks, sales quotes, sales order acknowledgements, sales invoices, sales credit memos, customer statements, customer past due letters, and customer return authorizations. Have several project team members review each document for accuracy and completeness.

Deployment

Transitioning to the New Software

Formally declare to the user community that there will be no software modifications made until after the first business cycle has been completed.

A good goal is to make zero modifications to the new software between end-user training and the closing of the first month's activity, which is typically completing the month-end process on the new software. The majority of issues and requests are most likely the result of users adjusting to the new software. There will inevitably be elements of the software that must be changed during this time, but changes should be made only when a user is prevented from successfully processing a required transaction or when a printed document is found to be incorrect or incomplete.

Deployment

Transitioning to the New Software

Document all issues discovered during deployment. Prioritize the issues if necessary.

After deploying the new software, track all issues reported by users on an issues list. This can be a handwritten list or a computerized spreadsheet. Only immediately resolve those issues that prevent users from processing transactions successfully. After thirty days, review the issues list to determine which issues are still open and which are no longer relevant. Also, for those that are still open, prioritize the order in which they will be addressed. The post-deployment period is when many organizations exceed their budget and spend significantly more than anticipated. The reason for this is that users are adjusting to the new software and are requesting changes to match the prior software. Be firm and require that users adapt to the new software prior to making modifications.

Deployment

Transitioning to the New Software

"Go-live" does not mean "finished."

The deployment phase does not end until every process has been completed in the new software at least once. The deployment process normally ends when all accounts in the general ledger have been reconciled in the financial statements and financial results have been completed for the first month of activity on the new software. Expect the first month-end to take longer than usual to complete due to the adjustments and training required internally to close the month. Allow for at least one to two weeks of additional time to produce the financial statements for the first month of activity. Finally, be prepared to utilize new reports that present information differently than the existing software. Ideally, there will be new, more insightful reports in the new software; however, if many custom reports were written in the existing software, these same reports may not be available in the new software without modification.

Deployment

Completing the Project and Next Steps

Meet with the project team to annouce the end of the implementation project.

Clearly defining the end of the initial deployment project is an important step, both organizationally and psychologically. While there will always be adjustments, monitoring, and training to be done, your team members will appreciate a formal closure to the project to bolster long-term confidence and signal a return to regular day-to-day productivity. This is also a great time to congratulate the team for a job well done and thank everyone for the additional effort given during the implementation project. Close the meeting by assuring the project team that all open issues will continue to be addressed and begin the process of prioritizing any new initiatives planned for the new software.

Deployment

Completing the Project and Next Steps

After the implementation is complete, provide a forum to allow team members to share their experiences on the project.

After the deployment phase is completed, formally meet with the project team to review and document the project successes and discuss lessons learned that can be applied to future phases of the existing project or to other projects taken on by the organization. It is important to document how the project was handled and what lessons were learned so that these concepts can be applied to the next software implementation, which will most likely occur within five to ten years. Share this information with the entire organization so that the lessons learned can be applied by other areas of the organization that may have their own software projects planned or already underway.

Deployment

Completing the Project and Next Steps

Maintain the project's momentum by immediately beginning the follow-up phases or project tasks.

Once the deployment phase is completed, immediately begin addressing the highest priority task on the follow-up phase/task list. This is critical to maintain project momentum and not stall the project before these follow-up phases are completed. While everyone would undoubtedly welcome a period of time to settle back into a "regular routine" after a long deployment project, delaying the follow-up phases/ tasks will only drag out the length of the project. It will also be harder to remotivate the project team after a period of inactivity. During the implementation period, a sense of "continuous improvement" was instilled in order to make sure that the organization was leveraging the software as much as possible. This attitude can be maintained by quickly moving forward to new initiatives and projects.

Deployment

Completing the Project and Next Steps

Expect ongoing maintenance and development costs with the new software.

All software requires ongoing maintenance, and this maintenance has a related cost. These costs are necessary to ensure that the latest technologies and tools are being utilized. In addition, maintaining the software is important so that new features can be implemented as your organization continues to change and grow over time. Thus, once the new software has been deployed and the first month has been closed, expect to regularly incur costs for the maintenance and continued development of the software. A good rule of thumb to use for annual maintenance and development costs is twenty-five percent of the initial purchase price of the software. This means that you will essentially be repurchasing the computer software every four years. But it will also allow you to leverage the new software to its fullest capabilities while not allowing your software to become quickly outdated and obsolete.

Summary and Final Thoughts

The implementation of accounting software is a major project that must be well organized and managed. This process begins with conducting a comprehensive evaluation to ensure that the software will meet the key requirements of the organization. Once you select the software, it is up to the project team to take ownership of it and ensure that training and implementation tasks occur in a timely fashion. The conversion of existing data can be a major implementation risk, so it is recommended that you manually enter as much data as possible and review the converted data thoroughly prior to deployment. Organizing a detailed deployment plan well in advance of the cutover to the new software will ensure that deployment of the new software goes as smoothly as possible. While the project will formally end, you will continue to see opportunities for improvement, and the organization should plan on continuous improvement and maintenance so that the software remains current for years to come. Ultimately, it is up to your organization and each of the project team members to take ownership of your new accounting system in order to make your implementation project a success.